THE

Prayer Tree

Leunig

Published by Collins Dove
A Division of HarperCollins*Publishers* (Australia) Pty Ltd
22-24 Joseph Street
North Blackburn, Victoria 3130

First published 1991
Designed by John Canty
Cover design by John Canty
Cover illustration Michael Leunig

Typeset in Bodoni by Evans Mason Services
Printed in Australia by Griffin Press Pty Ltd

The National Library of Australia
Cataloguing-in-Publication Data:
Leunig, Michael, 1945-
    The prayer tree.

    ISBN 1 86371 034 5.

    1. Prayers. 2. Meditations. I. Title.

242.8

INTRODUCTION

A person kneels to contemplate a tree and to reflect upon the troubles and joys of life.

*　　*　　*

It is difficult to accept that life is difficult; that love is not easy and that doubt and struggle, suffering and failure, are inevitable for each and every one of us.

We seek life's ease. We yearn for joy and release, for flowers and the sun. And although we may find these in abundance we also find ourselves lying awake at night possessed by the terrible fear that life is impossible. Sometimes when we least expect it we wake up overwhelmed by a massive sense of loneliness, misery, chaos and death: appalled by the agony and futility of existence.

It is difficult indeed to accept that this darkness belongs naturally and importantly to our human condition and that we must live with it and bear it. It seems so unbearable.

Nature, however, requires that we have the darkness of our painful feelings and that we respect it and make a bold place for it in our lives. Without its recognition and acceptance there can be no true sense of life's great depth, wherein lies our capacity to love, to create and to make meaning.

Nature requires that we form a relationship between our joy and our despair, that they not remain divided or hidden from one another. For these are the feelings which must cross-pollinate and inform each other in order that the soul be enlivened and strong. It is the soul, after all, which bears the burden of our experience. It is the soul through which we love and it is the soul which senses most faithfully our function within the integrity of the natural world.

Nature requires that we be soulful and therefore requires a dimension within us where darkness and light may meet and know each other. Mornings and evenings somewhere inside, with similar qualities to the mornings and the evenings of the earth. Qualities of gradual but vast change; of stillness and tender transference, fading and emerging, foreboding and revelation.

Mornings and evenings: the traditional times
for prayer and the singing of birds, times of
graceful light whereby the heart may envisage
its poetry and describe for us what it sees.

But how do we find the mornings and evenings
within? How do we establish and behold them
and be affected by their gentle atmospheres and
small miracles? How do we enter this healing
twilight?

The matter requires our imagination.
In particular, it requires the aspect of
imagination we have come to know as prayer.

We pray. We imagine our way inwards and
downwards and there, with heartfelt thoughts
or words we declare our fears and our
yearnings; we call out for love and forgiveness;
we proclaim our responsibility and gratitude.
The struggling, grounded soul speaks to the
higher spirit and thus we exist in the mornings
and the evenings of the heart: thus we are
affected and changed by the qualities we have
created within ourselves.

Might not prayer then be our most accessible

means to inner reconciliation; a natural healing function in response to the pain of the divided self and the divided world? Might not prayerfulness be part of our survival instinct belonging more to the wilderness than to the church.

And just as we have become somewhat alienated from nature and its cycles, could it be that we are also estranged from our instinctive capacity for prayer and need to understand it afresh from the example of the natural world?'

*   *   *

The person contemplates the tree.

*   *   *

The tree sends its roots beneath the surface, seeking nourishment in the dark soil: the rich "broken down" matter of life.

As they reach down and search, the roots hold the tree firmly to the earth.

Thus held and nourished, the tree grows upwards into the light, drinking the sun and air and expressing its truth: its branches and foliage, its flowers and fruit. Life swarms

around and into it. Birds and insects teem
within its embrace, carrying pollen and seed.
They nest and breed and sing and buzz.
They glorify the creation.

The tree changes as it grows. It is torn by
wind and lightning, scarred by frost and fire.
Branches die and new ones emerge. The
drama of existence has its way with the tree
but still it grows; still its roots reach down into
the darkness; still its branches flow with sap
and reach upward and outward into the world.

*   *   *

A person kneels to contemplate a tree and to
reflect upon the troubles and joys of life. The
person imagines mornings and evenings in a
great forest of prayers, swarming and teeming
with life.

The person is learning how to pray.

Love is born

With a dark and troubled face

When hope is dead

And in the most unlikely place

Love is born:

Love is always born.

God let us be serious.

Face to face.

Heart to heart.

Let us be fully present.

Strongly present.

Deeply serious.

The closest we may come

to innocence.

Amen

We welcome summer and the glorious
blessing of light. We are rich with light;
we are loved by the sun. Let us empty our
hearts into the brilliance. Let us pour our
darkness into the glorious, forgiving light.
For this loving abundance let us give thanks
and offer our joy.

Amen

We give thanks for the life and work of
Wolfgang Amadeus Mozart. Let us celebrate
and praise all those musicians and
composers who give their hands and hearts
and voices to the expression of life's mystery
and joy.

Who nourish our heart in its yearning.

Who dignify our soul in its struggling.

Who harmonise our grief and gladness.

Who make melody from the fragments
   of chaos.

Who align our spirit with creation.

Who reveal to us the grace of God.

Who calm us and delight us and set us free
    to love and forgive.
Let us give thanks and rejoice.

Amen

God bless our contradictions, those parts of us which seem out of character. Let us be boldly and gladly out of character. Let us be creatures of paradox and variety: creatures of contrast; of light and shade: creatures of faith. God be our constant. Let us step out of character into the unknown, to struggle and love and do what we will.

Amen

God help us with ideas, those thoughts which inform the way we live and the things we do. Let us not seize upon ideas, neither shall we hunt them down nor steal them away. Rather let us wait faithfully for them to approach, slowly and gently like creatures from the wild. And let them enter willingly into our hearts and come and go freely within the sanctuary of our contemplation, informing our souls as they arrive and being enlivened by the inspiration of our hearts as they leave.

These shall be our truest thoughts. Our willing and effective ideas. Let us treasure their humble originality. Let us follow them gently back into the world with faith that they shall lead us to lives of harmony and integrity.

Amen

God help us to find our confession;

The truth within us which is hidden from
  our mind;

The beauty or the ugliness we see elsewhere

But never in ourselves;

The stowaway which has been smuggled

Into the dark side of the heart,

Which puts the heart off balance and causes
  it pain,

Which wearies and confuses us,

Which tips us in false directions and inclines
  us to destruction,

The load which is not carried squarely

Because it is carried in ignorance.

God help us to find our confession.

Help us across the boundary of our
  understanding.

Lead us into the darkness that we may find
    what lies concealed;
That we may confess it towards the light;
That we may carry our truth in the centre
    of our heart;
That we may carry our cross wisely
And bring harmony into our life and
    our world.
Amen

God rest us.

Rest that part of us which is tired.

Awaken that part of us which is asleep.

God awaken us and awake within us.

Amen

We give thanks for the mystery of hair.

Too little here and too much there.

Censored and shaved, controlled and
 suppressed:

Unwelcome guest in soups and sandwiches.

Difficult growth always needing attention.

Gentle and comforting;

Complex and wild;

Reminding us softly

That we might be animals.

Growing and growing

'Til the day that we die.

And the day after as well

So they say!

In all of its places

And in all of its ways

We give thanks for the blessing of hair.

Amen

God be with those who explore in the cause of understanding; whose search takes them far from what is familiar and comfortable and leads them into danger or terrifying loneliness. Let us try to understand their sometimes strange or difficult ways; their confronting or unusual language; the uncommon life of their emotions, for they have been affected and shaped and changed by their struggle at the frontiers of a wild darkness, just as we may be affected, shaped and changed by the insights they bring back to us. Bless them with strength and peace.

Amen

God help us to live slowly:

To move simply:

To look softly:

To allow emptiness:

To let the heart create for us.

Amen

In order to be truthful

We must do more than speak the truth.

We must also hear truth.

We must also receive truth.

We must also act upon truth.

We must also search for truth.

The difficult truth.

Within us and around us.

We must devote ourselves to truth.

Otherwise we are dishonest

And our lives are mistaken.

God grant us the strength and the courage

To be truthful.

Amen

Dear God, we pray for another way of being: another way of knowing.

Across the difficult terrain of our existence we have attempted to build a highway and in so doing have lost our footpath. God lead us to our footpath: Lead us there where in simplicity we may move at the speed of natural creatures and feel the earth's love beneath our feet. Lead us there where step-by-step we may feel the movement of creation in our hearts. And lead us there where side-by-side we may feel the embrace

of the common soul. Nothing can be loved at speed. God lead us to the slow path; to the joyous insights of the pilgrim; another way of knowing: another way of being.

Amen

Let us live in such a way

That when we die

Our love will survive

And continue to grow.

Amen

God help us

To rise up from our struggle.

Like a tree rises up from the soil.

Our roots reaching down to our trouble,

Our rich, dark dirt of existence.

Finding nourishment deeply

And holding us firmly.

Always connected.

Growing upwards and into the sun.

Amen

Dear God,
We rejoice and give thanks for earthworms, bees, ladybirds and broody hens; for humans tending their gardens, talking to animals, cleaning their homes and singing to themselves; for the rising of the sap, the fragrance of growth, the invention of the wheelbarrow and the existence of the teapot, we give thanks. We celebrate and give thanks.
Amen

We give thanks for singers.

All types of singers.

Popular, concert singers and tuneless singers in the bath.

Whistlers, hummers and those who sing while they work.

Singers of lullabies; singers of nonsense and small scraps of melody.

Singers on branches and rooftops.

Morning yodellers and evening warblers.

Singers in seedy nightclubs, singers in the street;

Singers in cathedrals, school halls, grandstands, back yards, paddocks, bedrooms, corridors, stairwells and places of echo and resonance.

We give praise to all those who give some
    small voice
To the everyday joy of the soul.
Amen

We give thanks for the invention of the handle. Without it there would be many things we couldn't hold on to. As for the things we can't hold on to anyway, let us gracefully accept their ungraspable nature and celebrate all things elusive, fleeting and intangible. They mystify us and make us receptive to truth and beauty. We celebrate and give thanks.

Amen

God bless the lone tunnellers; those rare individuals whose joy and passion it is to dig mysterious tunnels beneath the surface of the earth; who share the soulful purpose of moles and worms; who labour gleefully beneath our feet while we bask in the sun or gaze at the stars; whose pockets and cuffs are full of soil; who dig faithfully in darkness, turning left and turning right, not knowing why or where, but absorbed and fulfilled nevertheless. Under houses; under roads and statues; beneath and amongst the roots of trees; on elbows and knees; carefully, steadily pawing at their beloved earth; sniffing and savouring the rich odour of the dirt; dreaming and delighting in the blackness; onwards and onwards, not

knowing day or night; unsung, unadorned, unassuming, unrestrained. Grimy fingernailed angels of the underworld: we praise them and give thanks for their constant, unseen presence and the vast labyrinth they have created beneath our existence. We praise them and give thanks. Amen

Autumn.

We give thanks for the harvest of the
heart's work;

Seeds of faith planted with faith;

Love nurtured by love;

Courage strengthened by courage.

We give thanks for the fruits of the
struggling soul,

The bitter and the sweet;

For that which has grown in adversity

And for that which has flourished in
warmth and grace;

For the radiance of the spirit in autumn

And for that which must now fade and die.

We are blessed and give thanks.

Amen

We give thanks for the blessing of winter:
Season to cherish the heart.
To make warmth and quiet for the heart.
To make soups and broths for the heart.
To cook for the heart and read for the
heart.
To curl up softly and nestle with the heart.
To sleep deeply and gently at one with
   the heart.
To dream with the heart.
To spend time with the heart.
A long, long time of peace with the heart.
We give thanks for the blessing of winter:
Season to cherish the heart.
Amen

God help us

If our world should grow dark;

And there is no way of seeing or knowing.

Grant us courage and trust

To touch and be touched

To find our way onwards

By feeling.

Amen

God bless those who suffer from the
   common cold.
Nature has entered into them;
Has led them aside and gently lain them low
To contemplate life from the wayside;
To consider human frailty;
To receive the deep and dreamy messages
   of fever.
We give thanks for the insights of this
   humble perspective.
We give thanks for blessings in disguise.
Amen

We simplify our lives.

We live gladly with less.

We let go the illusion that we can possess.

We create instead.

We let go the illusion of mobility.

We travel in stillness. We travel at home.

By candlelight and in stillness,

In the presence of flowers,

We make our pilgrimage.

We simplify our lives.

We give thanks for our friends.

Our dear friends.

We anger each other.

We fail each other.

We share this sad earth, this tender life,

   this precious time.

Such richness. Such wildness.

Together we are blown about.

Together we are dragged along.

All this delight.

All this suffering.

All this forgiving life.

We hold it together.

Amen

God bless this tiny little boat
And me who travels in it.
It stays afloat for years and years
And sinks within a minute.

And so the soul in which we sail,
Unknown by years of thinking,
Is deeply felt and understood
The minute that it's sinking.

We search and we search and yet find no
  meaning.

The search for a meaning leads to despair.

And when we are broken the heart finds its
  moment

To fly and to feel and to work as it will

Through the darkness and mystery and wild
  contradiction.

For this is its freedom, its need and its
  calling;

This is its magic, its strength and its
  knowing.

To heal and make meaning while we walk or
  lie dreaming;

To give birth to love within our surrender;

To mother our faith, our spirit and
  yearning;

While we stumble in darkness the heart
  makes our meaning
And offers it into our life and creation
That we may give meaning to life and
  creation
For we only give meaning we do not
  find meaning:
The thing we can't find is the thing we
  shall give.
To make love complete and to honour
  creation.

When the heart
Is cut or cracked or broken
Do not clutch it
Let the wound lie open

Let the wind
From the good old sea blow in
To bathe the wound with salt
And let it sting.

Let a stray dog lick it
Let a bird lean in the hole and sing
A simple song like a tiny bell
And let it ring

Let it go. Let it out.

Let it all unravel.

Let it free and it can be

A path on which to travel.